ARMOND
DALTON
PUBLISHERS
INC.

COMPUTERIZED ACCOUNTING

using QUICKBOOKS PRO 2018

FIFTH EDITION

Reference
Book 2 of 3

TABLE OF CONTENTS

Introduction

Purchases and Cash Disbursements Cycle Activities

TABLE OF CONTENTS (CONTINUED)

Sales and Cash Receipts Cycle Activities

Payroll Cycle and Other Activities

Introduction

Overview

The *QuickBooks* software is intended primarily for a wide variety of small and medium-size businesses and is therefore designed to accommodate many different circumstances. As a result, the software has dozens of windows and hundreds of boxes in which to enter or accept information.

To help students learn to use *QuickBooks*, the Reference book is a useful guide to correctly process transactions and do other activities. Based on experience with many students learning to use the software, those who follow the Reference book for each transaction or other activity perform better than those who do not. You will begin using the Reference book in Chapter 5 of the Instructions book.

The Reference book contains 25 sections, one for each transaction or other activity included in the *Computerized Accounting Using QuickBooks Pro 2018* project. See the table of contents on pages 1 and 2 for a list of the transactions and activities covered.

Contents of Reference Book

There are four parts to the Reference book:

1. **Inside Front Cover Listing of Transactions and Other Activities**—This listing can be used to help you locate the appropriate pages in the Reference book for recording transactions or doing other activities.

2. **Transaction or Other Activity Overview**—The brief overview describes what happens in *QuickBooks* for the transaction or other activity. The overview for each section is located above the Quick Reference Table.

3. **Quick Reference Table**—The Quick Reference Table is a guide to help you open the correct window(s) and enter or accept the correct information in each box.

4. **Window(s) on the Page Facing the Quick Reference Table**—You will be using these windows to process the transaction or other activity that you are dealing with. The circled letters on the window(s) match the steps on the Quick Reference Table. The letters will not appear on your screen.

Suggested Way To Use the Reference Book

The information in the Instructions book in Chapters 5 through 8 will direct you to the relevant Reference book pages. For each transaction or other activity you should first read the brief overview at the top of the page to help you understand what is happening in the *QuickBooks* software. Then follow the step-by-step instructions in the Quick Reference Table and related window or windows to process the transaction or complete the other activity.

For Chapters 9 and 10, you will not be told which pages include the relevant Quick Reference Table and related window or windows. For those transactions or other activities the following are suggestions to help you effectively use the Reference book:

- Determine the type of transaction or other activity you are to process. You will be able to make the determination using the information provided in the Instructions book and the knowledge gained in earlier chapters.

- Determine the applicable Reference book page numbers. You can locate the transaction or other activity on the inside front cover of the Reference book and determine the applicable page number.

- Open the Reference book to the pages for the transaction or other activity that you will be processing. Read the information in the brief overview at the top of the page to help you understand what is happening in the *QuickBooks* software

- Follow the step-by-step instructions in the Quick Reference Table and related window or windows to process the transaction or complete the other activity.

As you become proficient with *QuickBooks*, you may decide to process the transactions and other activities using the windows as guidance and refer to the Reference book only if you forget which window to use or the appropriate steps to follow. If you make an error, it is usually easy to correct it by either accessing the window again and correcting the information or deleting and reentering the transaction. Even if you follow that approach you will often find it useful to refer to the inside front cover of the Reference book to make sure you are processing the transaction or other activity in the correct window. You may also decide to follow the guidance in the Reference book for all transactions and other activities to minimize the likelihood of making errors.

This page is intentionally blank.

Prepare a Purchase Order

The purchase order window is used to prepare purchase orders for inventory. No accounting entry is made to any journal, subsidiary record, or general ledger after a purchase order is saved because a liability does not yet exist.

Quick Reference Table

Step	Box or Other Location	Procedure
A	Home Page	Click the Purchase Orders icon under Vendors.
B	Vendor	Select Vendor from drop-down list or add new. For a new vendor addition, refer to maintenance tasks in Chapter 5.
C	Date	Verify the date posted or enter new date.
D	P.O. No.	Accept the purchase order number or change.
E	Ship To	Accept the shipping address or change by typing in a different name and / or address.
F	Item	Select an item from drop-down list or add new item.
G	Description	Accept the default description or change.
H	Qty.	Enter the quantity to be ordered.
I	Rate	Accept the default rate or change.
J	Amount	Accept the total amount of the items ordered. Changing the amount column will recalculate the Rate.
K	Various	Repeat steps F – J for each inventory item to be ordered.
L	Create Purchase Orders window	Review the information to verify that it is correct.
M	Print button	Click the Print button, select the printer, and print the purchase order, if desired.
N	Save & Close / Save & New buttons	Click Save & Close or Save & New to save the purchase order.

Prepare a Purchase Order
QuickBooks windows

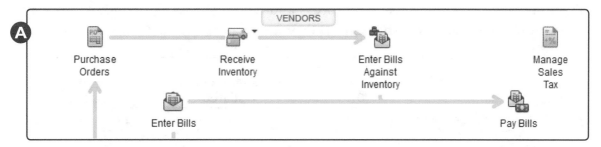

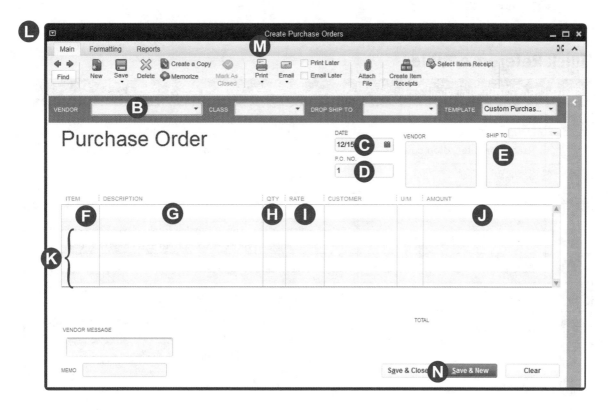

Receive Goods On a Purchase Order

The Enter Bills window is used to process and record the receipt of goods from an open purchase order. After the Enter Bills window is saved the following occurs:

Transactions	DR	CR	Subsidiary Records Updated	General Ledger Updated
Inventory, Fixed Assets, or Expenses	$		✓ (inventory and fixed assets)	✓
Accounts Payable		$	✓	✓

Quick Reference Table

Step	Box or Other Location	Procedure
A	Home Page	Click the Receive Inventory drop-down button under Vendors.
B	Receive Inventory drop-down list	Select "Receive Inventory with Bill" to open the Enter Bills window.
C	Vendor	Select a vendor from the drop-down list.
D	Open POs Exist window *(not shown)*	Click Yes.
E	Open Purchase Orders window	Select which purchase order is being received by placing a check mark on its line and click OK to return to Enter Bills window.
F	Date	Accept default date or change.
G	Ref No.	Type the vendor's invoice number.
H	Amount Due	Accept listed amount due or change. *(Not possible to verify unless the information is provided.)*
I	Terms	Accept the default terms or select from the drop-down list.
J	Items tab	Click to open the Items tab if it is not open.
K	Item	For each item, accept the items ordered or change using the drop-down list.
L	Description	Accept the default description or edit.
M	Qty.	For each item type received, accept the quantity ordered or change to the quantity that was received.
N	Cost	For each item received, accept default cost or change.
O	Expenses tab *(content not shown)*	Click the Expenses tab. Verify that correct general ledger account is in Account Box, type the sales tax amount in the Amount Box, then type "Sales Tax" in the Memo box.
P	Enter Bills window	Review the information to verify that it is correct.
Q	Save & Close / Save & New buttons	Click Save & Close or Save & New button.

Receive Goods On a Purchase Order
QuickBooks windows

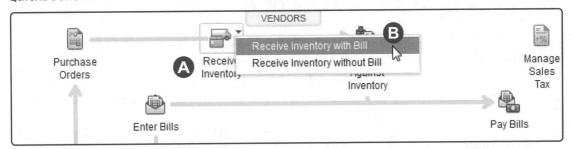

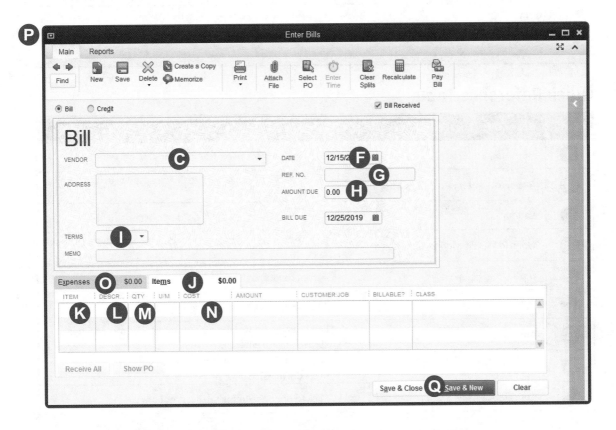

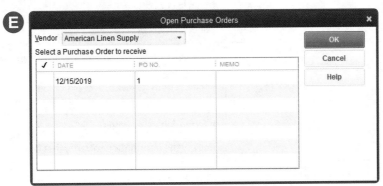

Purchase Inventory Without a Purchase Order—No Payment Made at Time of Purchase

The Enter Bills window is used to process and record the receipt of goods purchased without a purchase order. After entering information and saving the completed Enter Bills window, the following has occurred:

Transactions	DR	CR	Subsidiary Records Updated	General Ledger Updated
Inventory	$		✓	✓
Accounts Payable		$	✓	✓

Quick Reference Table

Step	Box or Other Location	Procedure
A	Home Page	Click the Receive Inventory icon under Vendors.
B	Receive Inventory drop-down list	Select Receive Inventory with Bill (not shown) to open the Enter Bills window.
C	Vendor	Select a vendor from the drop-down list or add new.
D	Open POs Exist window (not shown)	If there are open POs for this vendor, this window will open. Click No.
E	Date	Accept default date or change.
F	Ref No.	Type the vendor's invoice number.
G	Amount Due	Leave blank. Information is automatically entered when steps J–M are entered.
H	Terms	Accept the default payment terms or select from the drop-down list.
I	Items tab	Click to open the Items tab if it is not open.
J	Item	For each item, select the items received from the drop-down list or add new.
K	Description	For each item, accept the default description or edit.
L	Qty.	For each item, enter the quantity of items received.
M	Cost	For each item received, accept default cost or change.
N	Amount	Verify the total is correct. (Not possible to verify unless the information is provided.)
O	Enter Bills window	Review the information to verify that it is correct.
P	Save & Close / Save & New buttons	Click the Save & Close or Save & New button.

Purchase Inventory Without a Purchase Order—
No Payment Made At Time of Purchase

QuickBooks windows

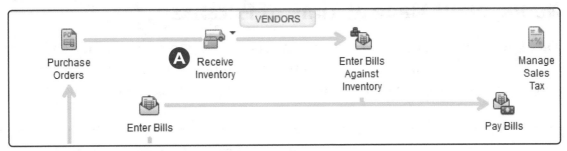

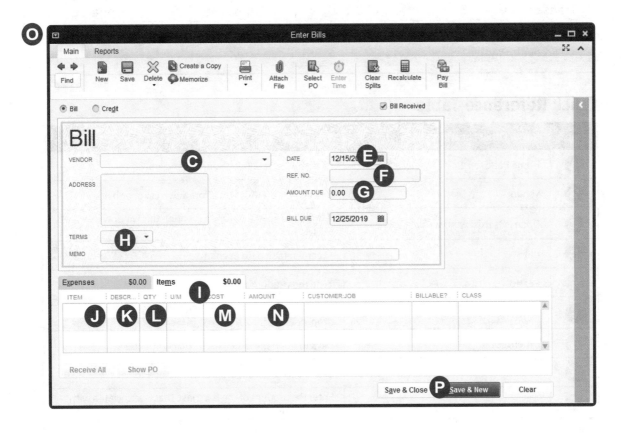

Purchase Non-Inventory Items or Services Without a Purchase Order— No Payment Made at Time of Purchase

The Enter Bills window is used to process and record the receipt of non-inventory items or services purchased without a purchase order. After entering information and saving the completed Enter Bills window, the following has occurred:

Transactions	DR	CR	Subsidiary Records Updated	General Ledger Updated
Expense and Non-Inv. Asset Accounts	$		✓ (fixed assets)	✓
Accounts Payable		$	✓	✓

Quick Reference Table

Step	Box or Other Location	Procedure
A	Home Page	Click the Enter Bills icon under Vendors.
B	Vendor	Select a vendor from the drop-down list or add new.
C	Open POs Exist window (not shown)	If there are open POs for this vendor, this window will open. Click No.
D	Date	Accept default date or change.
E	Ref No.	Type the vendor's invoice number.
F	Terms	Accept the default payment terms or select from the drop-down list.
G	Expenses tab	Click to open the Expenses tab if it is not open.
H	Account	Select account from drop-down list or add new.
I	Amount	Enter the amount of the purchase that is associated with the account.
J	Memo	Type a description of the amount that is being charged to the account (legal services, for example).
K	Various	Repeat steps H – J for any other accounts that are applicable to the purchase.
L	Amount Due	Verify that the amount due is correct. (Not possible to verify unless the information is provided.)
M	Enter Bills window	Review the information to verify that it is correct.
N	Save & Close / Save & New buttons	Click the Save & Close or Save & New button.

Purchase Non-Inventory Items or Services Without a Purchase Order— No Payment Made At Time of Purchase

QuickBooks windows

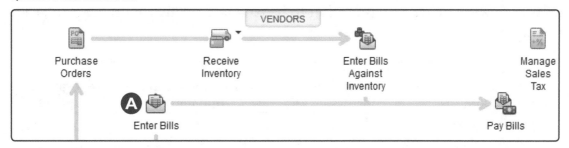

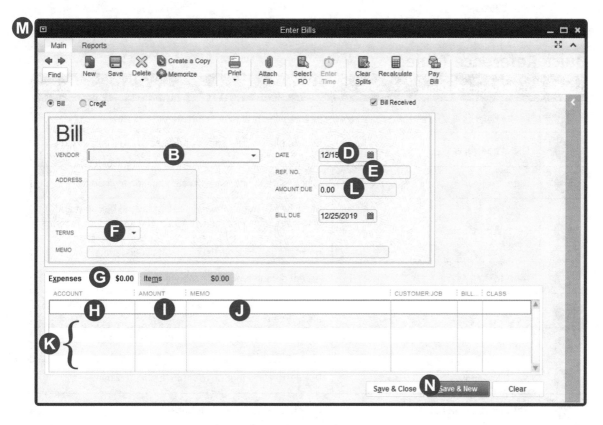

Pay a Vendor's Outstanding Invoice

The Pay Bills window is used to record and process a payment for a vendor's existing invoice. After selecting a bill to be paid and saving the transaction, the following has occurred:

Transactions	DR	CR	Subsidiary Records Updated	General Ledger Updated
Accounts Payable	$		✓	✓
Accounts Payable		$		✓
Discount/Credit		$		✓

Quick Reference Table

Step	Box or Other Location	Procedure
A	Home Page	Click the Pay Bills icon under Vendors.
B	List of open bills	Click to place a checkmark and select the bill or bills to be paid.
C	Date	Accept default date or click calendar icon to change.
D	Set Discount button	Click the Set Discount button to display the Discount and Credits window (not shown). Accept the Amount of Discount and the Discount Account or edit. (Note: Discounts are not normally given for partial payments.) Click Done.
E	Amt. To Pay	Accept default amount or change for a partial payment.
F	Assign check number button	Select the Assign check number radio button if it is not already selected.
G	Method	Accept the default payment method or change from the drop-down list.
H	Pay Bills window	Review the information to verify that it is correct.
I	Pay Selected Bills button	Click the Pay Selected Bills button.
J	Check No. box (Assign Check Numbers window)	Type check number and click the OK button.
K	Payment Summary window	Review the information to verify that it is correct.
L	Done button (Payment Summary window)	Click the Done button to exit to the Home Page.

Pay a Vendor's Outstanding Invoice
QuickBooks windows

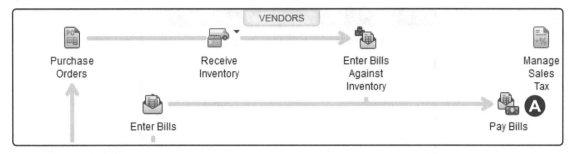

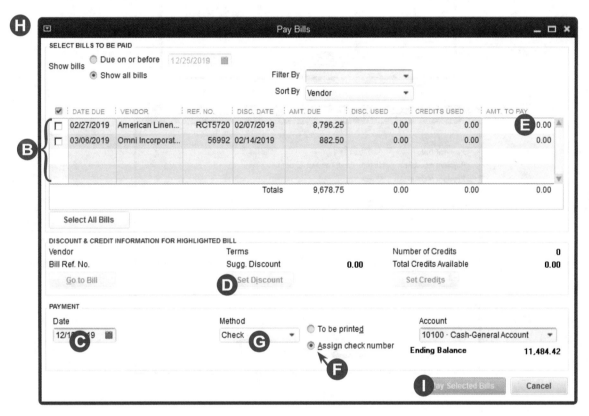

(windows continued on the following page)

Pay a Vendor's Outstanding Invoice

QuickBooks windows *(continued)*

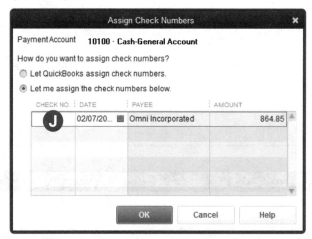

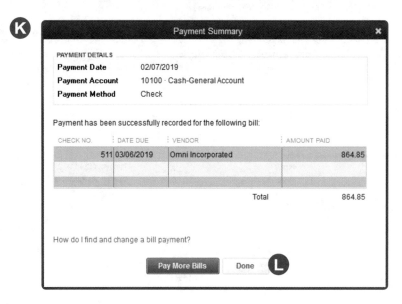

This page is intentionally blank.

Purchase Inventory Without a Purchase Order— Payment Made at Time of Purchase

The Write Checks window is used to process and record purchases without a recorded purchase order that are paid at the time of the purchase. After the Write Checks window is saved, the following has occurred:

Transactions	DR	CR	Subsidiary Records Updated	General Ledger Updated
Inventory	$		✓	✓
Checking Account		$		✓

Quick Reference Table

Step	Box or Other Location	Procedure
A	Home Page	Click the Write Checks icon under Banking.
B	No.	Accept default or enter the correct check number.
C	Date	Accept default date or change.
D	Pay to the Order of	Click the drop-down list arrow and select vendor or add new.
E	Open POs Exist window (not shown)	If there are open POs for this vendor, this window will open. Click No.
F	Continue Writing Check button (Open Bills Exist window - not shown)	If there are open bills for this vendor, the Open Bills Exist window will open. Click the Continue Writing Check button to return to the Write Checks window.
G	Memo	Enter the vendor invoice number.
H	Items tab	Click the Items tab if it is not already open.
I	Item	Select the first item from drop-down list or add new.
J	Description	Accept default description or edit.
K	Qty.	Enter the quantity purchased.
L	Cost	Accept the default cost or edit.
M	Various	Repeat steps I–L for each inventory item purchased.
N	$	Verify the total amount of the check. (Not possible to verify unless the information is provided.)
O	Write Checks window	Review the information to verify that it is correct.
P	Save & Close / Save & New buttons	Click the Save & Close or Save & New button.

Purchase Inventory Without a Purchase Order—Payment Made At Time of Purchase

QuickBooks windows

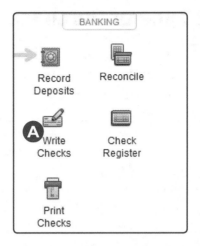

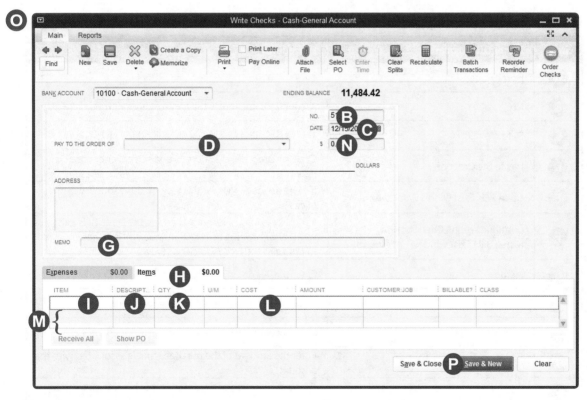

Purchase Non-Inventory Items or Services Without a Purchase Order— Payment Made at Time of Purchase

The Write Checks window is used to process and record purchases without a recorded purchase order that are paid at the time of the purchase. After the Write Checks window is saved, the following has occurred:

Transactions	DR	CR	Subsidiary Records Updated	General Ledger Updated
Various Exp. or Non-Inv. Asset Accounts	$		✓ (fixed assets)	✓
Checking Account		$		✓

Quick Reference Table

Step	Box or Other Location	Procedure
A	Home Page	Click the Write Checks icon under Banking.
B	No.	Accept default or enter the correct check number.
C	Date	Accept default date or click the calendar icon to change.
D	Pay to the Order of	Click the drop-down list arrow and select vendor or add new.
E	Open POs Exist window *(not shown)*	If there are open POs for this vendor, this window will open. Click No.
F	Continue Writing Check button (Open Bills Exist window - *not shown*)	If there are open bills for this vendor, the Open Bills Exist window will open. Click the Continue Writing Check button to return to the Write Checks window.
G	Memo	Enter the vendor invoice number.
H	Expenses tab	Click the Expenses tab if it is not already open.
I	Account	Select account from the drop-down list or add new.
J	Amount	Enter the amount of the purchase that is associated with the account.
K	Memo	Type a description of the amount that is being charged to the account.
L	Various	Repeat steps I–K for any other accounts applicable to the purchase.
M	$	Verify the total amount of the check. *(Not possible to verify unless the information is provided.)*
N	Write Checks window	Review the information to verify that it is correct.
O	Save & Close / Save & New buttons	Click the Save & Close or Save & New button.

Purchase Non-Inventory Items or Services Without a Purchase Order— Payment Made At Time of Purchase

QuickBooks windows

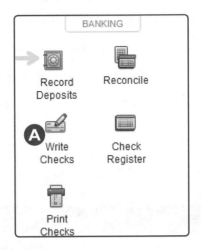

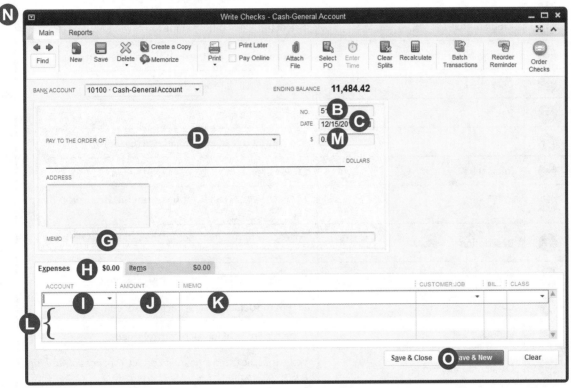

Return Inventory From a Purchase

The Enter Bills window is used to record and process returns made from purchases. After entering the credit information and saving, the following has occurred:

Transactions	DR	CR	Subsidiary Records Updated	General Ledger Updated
Accounts Payable	$		✓	✓
Inventory		$	✓	✓

Quick Reference Table

Step	Box or Other Location	Procedure
A	Home Page	Click the Enter Bills icon under Vendors.
B	Credit button	Select the Credit button at the top of window.
C	Vendor	Select a vendor from the drop-down list or add new.
D	Date	Accept default date or change.
E	Ref. No.	Type the debit memo number.
F	Memo	Type the invoice number related to the return.
G	Items tab	Click the Items tab if it is not already open.
H	Item	For each item, select items being returned from drop-down list.
I	Description	For each returned item, accept the default description or edit.
J	Qty.	For each item, enter the quantity being returned.
K	Cost	Accept the default cost for each item or edit.
L	Various	Repeat steps H – K for each item returned
M	Credit Amount	Verify that the listed amount is correct. *(Not possible to verify unless information is provided.)*
N	Enter Bills window	Review the information to verify that it is correct.
O	Save & Close / Save & New buttons	Click the Save & Close or Save & New button.

Return Inventory From a Purchase
QuickBooks windows

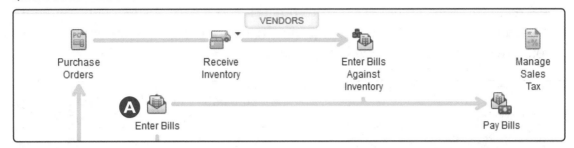

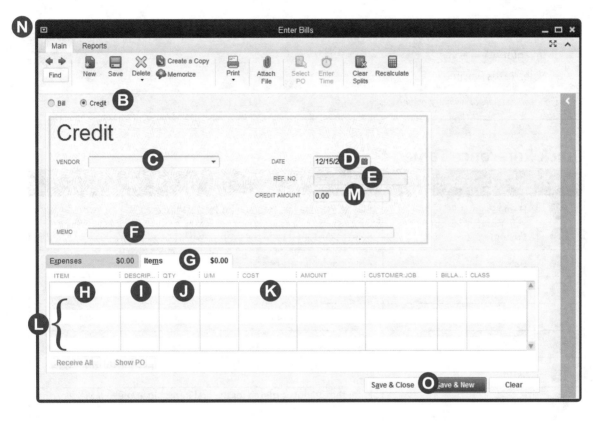

Make a Credit Sale

The Create Invoices window is used to process and record a sale when payment is expected in the future. After entering information and saving the completed Create Invoices window, the following has occurred:

Transactions	DR	CR	Subsidiary Records Updated	General Ledger Updated
Accounts Receivable	$		✓	✓
Cost of Goods Sold*	$			✓*
Sales Revenue		$		✓
Inventory*		$	✓*	✓*
Sales Taxes Payable		$		✓

Applies only to sales of inventory, not services.

Quick Reference Table

Step	Box or Other Location	Procedure
A	Home Page	Click the Create Invoices icon under Customers.
B	Customer: Job	Select a customer from the drop-down list or add new.
C	Date	Accept default date or edit.
D	Invoice #	Accept default number or edit.
E	Bill To	Verify that the correct customer information is displayed or edit.
F	P.O. Number	Enter the customer purchase order number.
G	Terms	Accept the default terms or select different terms from the drop-down list.
H	Quantity	Enter the quantity ordered for the first item sold. (Note that the item code will be entered next.)
I	Item Code	For the first item sold, select the item from the drop-down list or add new.
J	Description	Accept the default description or edit.
K	Price Each	Accept the default price or edit.
L	Various	Repeat steps H–K for each inventory item sold.
M	Balance Due	Verify that the balance due is correct. (Not possible to verify unless information is provided.)
N	Create Invoices–Accounts Receivable window	Review the information to verify that it is correct.
O	Print button	Select the print button at the top of the window only if the invoice is to be printed.
P	Save & Close / Save & New buttons	Click the Save & Close or Save & New button.

Make a Credit Sale

QuickBooks windows

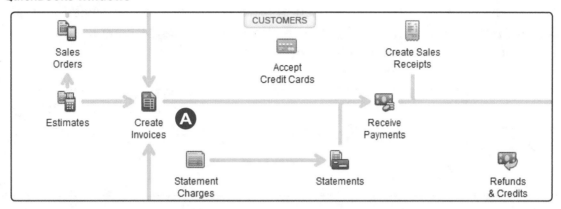

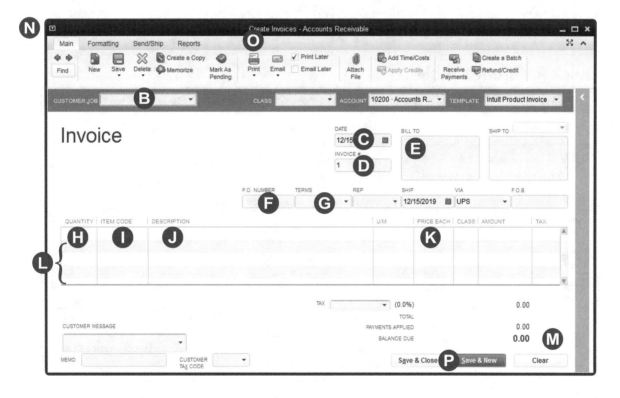

Collect an Account Receivable

The Receive Payments window is used to process and record the collection of an account receivable. After entering information and saving the completed Receive Payments window, the following has occurred:

Transactions	DR	CR	Subsidiary Records Updated	General Ledger Updated
Undeposited Funds	$			✓
Accounts Receivable		$	✓	✓

QuickBooks keeps track of money received in the Undeposited Funds Account. Money is kept in the fund until it is deposited into the bank.

Quick Reference Table

Step	Box or Other Location	Procedure
A	Home Page	Click the Receive Payments icon under Customers.
B	Received From	Select a customer from the drop-down list.
C	Invoice number line being paid	Highlight anywhere on the relevant invoice number line. (Skip this step if it is the only item or top item on the list.)
D	Payment Amount	Enter the amount of collection.
E	Date	Accept default date or change.
F	Payment Method buttons	Select the payment method using one of the available buttons or select an alternative using the More drop-down list.
G	Reference # / Check #	Enter the check number if payment method is a check or enter another number for alternate methods, such as credit card # for credit card receipts. Note that if you selected Check in step F, the Reference # box title changes to Check #.
H	Discount and Credits button	Click the Discount and Credits button to display the Discount and Credits window, then click the Discount tab if it is not already open.
I	Discount and Credits window	Verify that the applicable discount (amount and account) is correct or change and click the Done button to return to the Receive Payments window, then click the Discount tab if it is not already open.
J	Receive Payments window	Review the information to verify that it is correct.
K	Print button	Select the Print button at the top of the window if the receipt is to be printed.
L	Save & Close / Save & New buttons	Click the Save & Close or Save & New button.

Collect an Account Receivable
QuickBooks windows

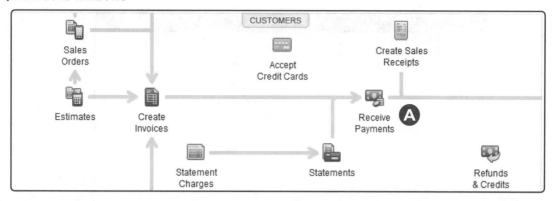

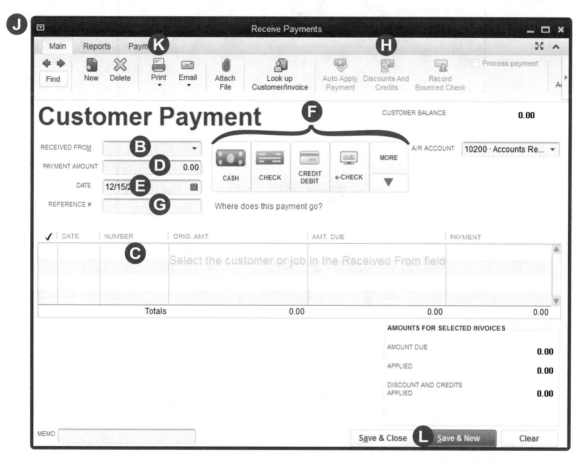

(windows continued on the following page)

Collect an Account Receivable

QuickBooks windows *(continued)*

This page is intentionally blank.

Make a Deposit

The Record Deposits window is used to record deposits into one of the company's bank accounts. After the payment information has been updated and saved, the following had occurred:

Transactions	DR	CR	Subsidiary Records Updated	General Ledger Updated
Checking Account	$			✓
Undeposited Funds		$		✓

Quick Reference Table

Step	Box or Other Location	Procedure
A	Home Page	Click the Record Deposits icon under Banking.
B	Payments to Deposit window	Click anywhere on the line to mark each payment to be deposited and click the OK button to open the Make Deposits window.
C	Date	Accept the default date or enter the correct date of the deposit.
D	Make Deposits window	Review the information to verify that it is correct.
E	Print button	Select the Print button at the top of the window if the deposit is to be printed.
F	Save & Close / Save & New buttons	Click the Save & Close or Save & New button.

Make a Deposit

QuickBooks windows

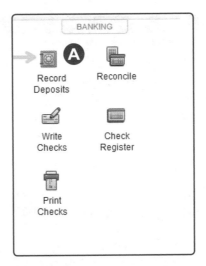

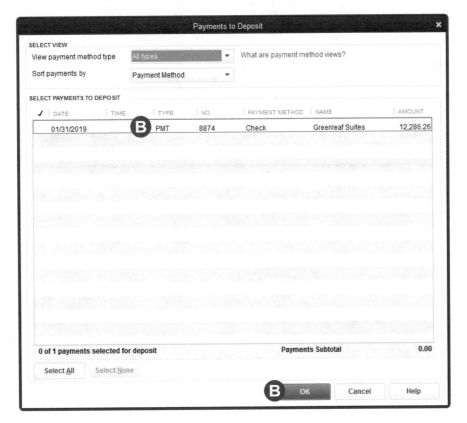

(windows continued on the following page)

Reference — Sales and Cash Receipts Cycle Activities

Make a Deposit
QuickBooks windows *(continued)*

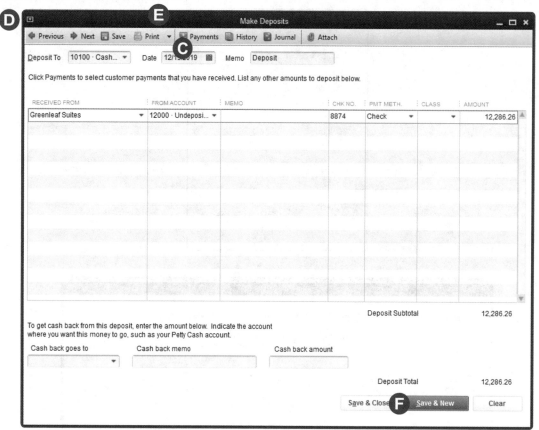

This page is intentionally blank.

Make a Cash Sale

The Create Sales Receipts window is used to process and record receipts of cash sales to customers. After the sales receipt information has been updated and saved, the following has occurred:

Transactions	DR	CR	Subsidiary Records Updated	General Ledger Updated
Undeposited Funds	$			✓
Cost of Goods Sold*	$			✓*
Sales Revenue		$		✓
Inventory*		$	✓*	✓*
Sales Taxes Payable		$		✓

Applies only to sales of inventory, not services.

QuickBooks keeps track of money received in the Undeposited Funds Account. Money is kept in the fund until it is deposited into the bank.

Quick Reference Table

Step	Box or Other Location	Procedure
A	Home Page	Click the Create Sales Receipts icon under Customers.
B	Customer: Job	Select a customer from the drop-down list or add new. For cash customers not in AR subsidiary records, select customer ID for cash customer.
C	Payment Method buttons	Select the payment method using one of the available buttons or select an alternative using the More drop-down list.
D	Date	Accept default date or edit.
E	Sale No.	Accept the default number or enter the cash sale invoice number.
F	Sold To	Verify the customer information is correct or edit. For cash customers not in AR subsidiary records, type customer information.
G	Check No.	Enter the customer's check number.
H	Item	For the first item sold, select the item from the drop-down list or add new.
I	Description	Accept the default description or edit.
J	Qty.	Enter the quantity sold.
K	Rate	Accept the default rate or enter the correct rate.
L	Amount	Accept the default amount or edit.

(table continued on the following page)

Quick Reference Table *(continued)*

Step	Box or Other Location	Procedure
M	Various	Repeat steps H – L for each inventory item sold.
N	Total	Verify that the amount is correct. *(Not possible to verify unless information is provided).*
O	Enter Sales Receipts window	Review the information to verify that it is correct.
P	Print button	Select the print button at the top of the window if the invoice is to be printed.
Q	Save & Close / Save & New buttons	Click the Save & Close or Save & New button. If you receive a message about changing the billing address for cash customers, click No.

Make a Cash Sale

QuickBooks windows

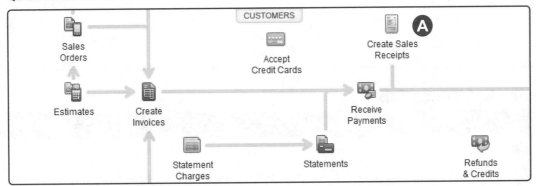

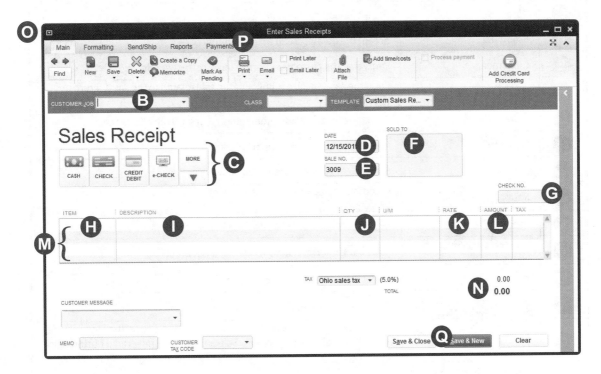

Process a Sales Return or Allowance (Credit Memo)

The Create Credit Memos/Refunds window is used to process credit memos for returns and allowances to customers. After the sales receipt information has been updated and saved, the following has occurred:

Transactions	DR	CR	Subsidiary Records Updated	General Ledger Updated
Sales Returns & Allowance	$			✓
Inventory*	$		✓*	✓*
Sales Taxes Payable	$			✓
Accounts Receivable		$	✓	✓
Cost of Goods Sold*		$		✓*

*Applies only to returns, not allowances.

Quick Reference Table

Step	Box or Other Location	Procedure
A	Home Page	Click the Refunds & Credits icon under Customers.
B	Customer: Job	Select a customer from the drop-down list or add new.
C	Date	Accept default date or edit.
D	Credit No.	Accept the default credit memo number or edit.
E	Customer	Verify that the customer information is correct or edit.
F	P.O. No.	Enter the sales invoice number of the sale related to the sales return or allowance.
G	Item	Select the first inventory item returned or given an allowance.
H	Description	Accept the default description or edit
I	Qty.	Enter the quantity returned. For allowances, leave blank.
J	Rate	Accept the default rate or edit. For allowances, enter the amount of the allowance.
K	Various	Repeat steps G – J for each inventory item returned.
L	Create Memos/Refunds window	Review the information to verify that it is correct.
M	Print button	Select the print button to print a receipt.
N	Save & Close/ Save & New buttons	Click the Save & Close or Save & New button.
O	Available Credit message (not shown)	When the customer has an Accounts Receivable balance, the Available Credit message opens. Select the appropriate radio button. Click OK. For Apply to an invoice, the Apply Credit to Invoices window opens.
P	Apply Credit to Invoices window (not shown)	Highlight anywhere on the relevant invoice number line. Click Done.

Process a Sales Return or Allowance (Credit Memo)

QuickBooks windows

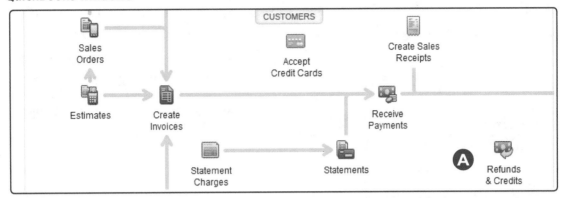

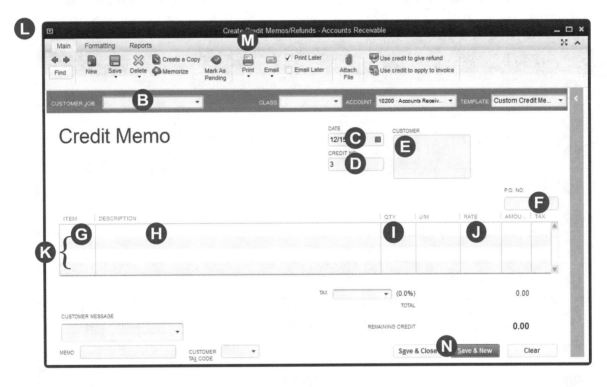

Write Off an Uncollectible Account Receivable

The Receive Payments window is used to process and record write off of accounts receivable that are uncollectible. After the write-off information has been updated and saved, the following has occurred:

Transactions	DR	CR	Subsidiary Records Updated	General Ledger Updated
Bad Debt Expense	$			✓
Accounts Receivable		$	✓	✓

Quick Reference Table

Step	Box or Other Location	Procedure
A	Home Page	Click the Receive Payments icon under Customers.
B	Received From	Select a customer from the drop-down list.
C	Payment Amount	Accept the "0.00" default.
D	Date	Accept the default date or edit.
E	Payment Method buttons	Select the Cash button.
F	Reference #	Type "write off."
G	Invoice number line being written off	Highlight anywhere on the relevant invoice number line. *(Skip this step if it is the only item or top item on the list.)*
H	Discount and Credits button	Click the Discount and Credits button to open the Discounts and Credits window, then click the Discount tab if it is not already open.
I	Amount of Discount	Enter the amount to be written off.
J	Discount Account	Select the Bad Debt Expense account from the drop-down list.
K	Discount and Credits window	Verify that the information entered is correct and click the Done button to return to the Receive Payments window.
L	Receive Payments window	Review the information to verify that it is correct.
M	Print button	Select the Print button to print the receipt.
N	Save & Close / Save & New buttons	Click the Save & Close or Save & New button.

Write Off an Uncollectible Account Receivable
QuickBooks windows

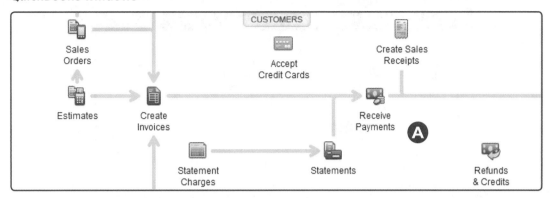

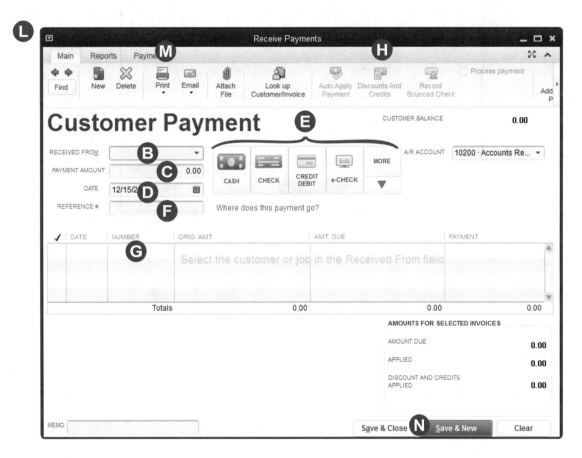

(windows continued on the following page)

Write Off an Uncollectible Account Receivable

QuickBooks windows *(continued)*

This page is intentionally blank.

Receive a Miscellaneous Cash Receipt

The Make Deposits window is used to process and record miscellaneous cash receipts. After the credit account is selected and the information completed, the following has occurred:

Transactions	DR	CR	Subsidiary Records Updated	General Ledger Updated
Undeposited Cash	$			✓
Applicable accounts*		$		✓*

*Examples include Notes Payable (new loans), Property Plant and Equipment (sales for cash), Marketable Securities (sales), Interest Income, and Miscellaneous Income.

QuickBooks keeps track of money received in the Undeposited Funds Account. Money is kept in the fund until it is deposited into the bank.

Quick Reference Table

Step	Box or Other Location	Procedure
A	Home Page	Click the Record Deposits icon under Banking. If the Payments to Deposit window opens *(not shown)*, click Cancel. A Make Deposits window opens next.
B	Date	Accept the default date or edit.
C	Received From	Select an existing customer or vendor from the drop-down list or add new.**
D	From Account	Select the account to be credited from the drop-down list.
E	Memo	Enter descriptive information about the receipt.
F	Chk No.	If payment method was a check, enter the check number.
G	Pmt Meth.	Select the payment method from the drop-down list.
H	Amount	Enter the amount of the receipt.
I	Various	Repeat steps C–H on the next line if more than one account is to be credited.
J	Make Deposits window	Review the information to verify that it is correct.
K	Print button	Select the Print button at the top of the window if deposit is to be printed.
L	Save & Close / Save & New buttons	Click the Save & Close or Save & New button.

**For a new "Received From" source, Click <Add New> at the top of the drop-down list to open the Select Name Type window. Click the appropriate type and then OK to open the relevant maintenance window. Complete the maintenance window and save the information to proceed with the remaining steps to Receive a Miscellaneous Cash Receipt.

Receive a Miscellaneous Cash Receipt

QuickBooks windows

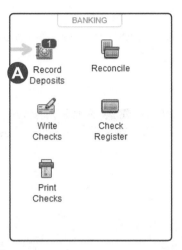

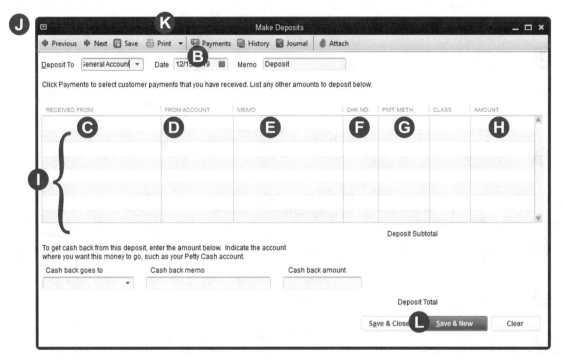

Prepare a Statement for Accounts Receivable

The Create Statements window is used to create various account statements, including an Accounts Receivable Statement, which can then be sent to a customer. No accounting entries occur.

Quick Reference Table

Step	Box or Other Location	Procedure
A	Home Page	Click the Statements icon under Customers.
B	Statement Date	Accept the end of period default date or edit.
C	Statement Period From and To –or– All open transactions as of Statement Date	Accept the default radio button setting or select the next option.
D	Statement Period From and To (If another radio button is selected, skip this step.)	Accept the default dates to create a monthly statement or change dates.
E	Select Customers	Accept the default All Customers setting or select the desired radio button. **For Multiple Customers,** click the Multiple Customers radio button, click the Choose button, and select the desired customers in the Print Statements window, then click OK *(not shown)*. **For One Customer,** click the One Customer radio button, then select the customer from the drop-down list *(not shown)*.
F	Select Additional Options	Complete this section by adding and/or removing check marks to be consistent with the information that is to be included in the customer statement(s).
G	Preview button	Click the Preview button to verify that the information displayed is correct. Then click the Close button to return to the Create Statements window.
H	Print / Close buttons	Click the Print button if a printout is desired, or click the Close button.

Prepare a Statement for Accounts Receivable

QuickBooks windows

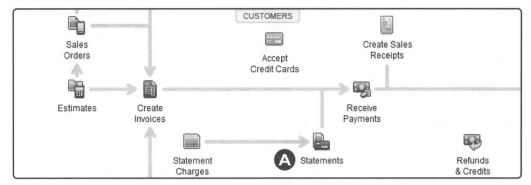

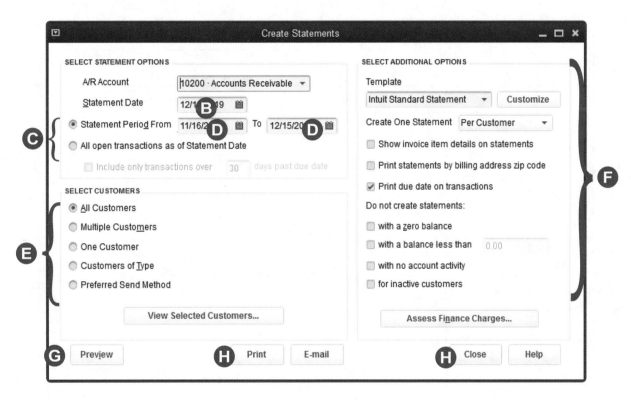

(windows continued on the following page)

Prepare a Statement for Accounts Receivable

QuickBooks **windows** *(continued)*

Jackson Supply Company

6211 Washburn Ave.
Columbus, OH 43216
(555) 342-4500

Statement

Date
12/31/2019

To:
McCarthy's B&B 511 Mansion Columbus, OH 43216

Amount Due	Amount Enc.
$3,138.75	

U/M	Date	Transaction	Amount	Balance
	11/30/2019	Balance forward		3,138.75

CURRENT	1-30 DAYS PAST DUE	31-60 DAYS PAST DUE	61-90 DAYS PAST DUE	OVER 90 DAYS PAST DUE	Amount Due
0.00	0.00	0.00	0.00	3,138.75	$3,138.75

This page is intentionally blank.

Pay Employees

The Review and Create Paychecks window is used to record payroll checks to employees. After entering information and creating employee paychecks, the following has occurred:

Transactions	DR	CR	Subsidiary Records Updated	General Ledger Updated
Salary and Wages Expense	$		✓	✓
Payroll Tax Expense (Employer Portion)	$			✓
Payroll Tax Withholdings and Other Employee Reductions		$	✓	✓
Payroll Tax Liabilities (Employer Portion)		$		✓
Cash		$		✓

Quick Reference Table

Step	Box or Other Location	Procedure
A	Home Page	Click the Pay Employees icon under Employees.
B	Start Unscheduled Payroll button	Select the Payroll tab and click Start Unscheduled Payroll to open the Enter Payroll Information window.
C	Pay Period Ends	Verify the date entered or change.
D	Check Date	Verify check date or change.
E	Handwrite & Assign check numbers radio button	Click the radio button if it is not already selected. Note that you will not be printing checks in this project, so you need to select the manual check option. *QuickBooks* will record the effects of the paychecks, but you will not have to print them.
F	First Check # box	Accept the default check number or change.
G	Check All button	Click the Check All button to select all employees. *Note:* If you are only paying one employee, click only on that employee's line, which will place a check mark next to the employee's name.
H	Regular Pay and Overtime hours boxes	Enter the regular pay hours and overtime hours for each hourly employee in the window.
I	Continue button	Click the Continue button to open the Review and Create Paychecks window.
J	Open Paycheck Detail button	Click the Open Paycheck Detail button to open the Preview Paycheck window for the first employee.
K	Preview Paycheck window	Review the information entered under Earnings and other payroll items. Accept the default information or edit the rate, hours, etc. Click Save & Next.

(table continued on the following page)

Quick Reference Table *(continued)*

Step	Box or Other Location	Procedure
L	Preview Paycheck window	Repeat step K for all remaining employees. When you have reviewed the last employee's paycheck, click Save & Close instead of Save & Next. This reopens the Review and Create Paychecks window.
M	Review and Create Paychecks window	Verify that all entered information is correct. If correct, click the Create Paychecks button. If there are errors, correct them in this window or use the Open Paycheck Detail button to open the Preview Paycheck Detail window and correct the information.
N	Confirmation and Next Steps window	Click Close. Note that in this project you will not be printing paychecks, so there is no need to select the Print Paychecks button.

Pay Employees

QuickBooks windows

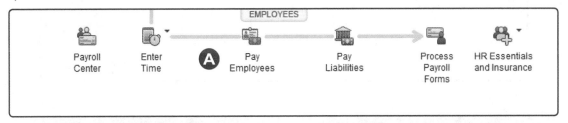

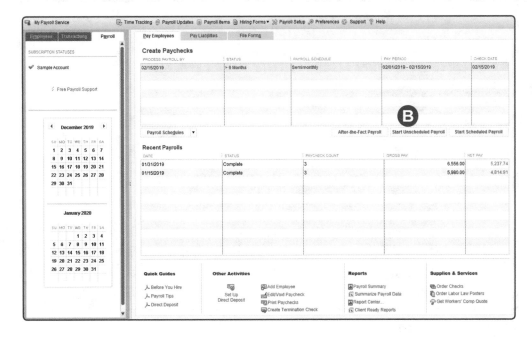

(windows continued on the following page)

Pay Employees

QuickBooks windows *(continued)*

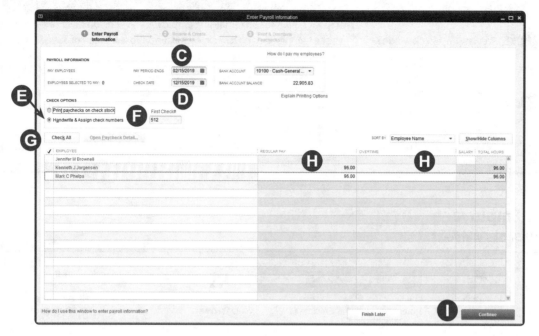

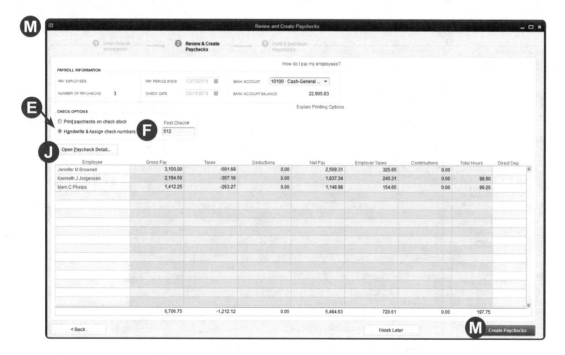

(windows continued on the following page)

Pay Employees

QuickBooks windows *(continued)*

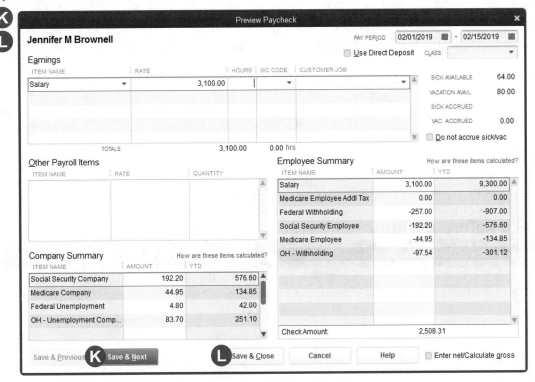

K
L

Preview Paycheck

Jennifer M Brownell

PAY PERIOD 02/01/2019 - 02/15/2019

☐ Use Direct Deposit   CLASS

Earnings

ITEM NAME	RATE	HOURS	WC CODE	CUSTOMER:JOB
Salary	3,100.00			

TOTALS	3,100.00	0.00 hrs	

SICK AVAILABLE 64.00
VACATION AVAIL. 80.00
SICK ACCRUED
VAC. ACCRUED 0.00
☐ Do not accrue sick/vac

Other Payroll Items

ITEM NAME	RATE	QUANTITY

Employee Summary   How are these items calculated?

ITEM NAME	AMOUNT	YTD
Salary	3,100.00	9,300.00
Medicare Employee Addl Tax	0.00	0.00
Federal Withholding	-257.00	-907.00
Social Security Employee	-192.20	-576.60
Medicare Employee	-44.95	-134.85
OH - Withholding	-97.54	-301.12

Company Summary   How are these items calculated?

ITEM NAME	AMOUNT	YTD
Social Security Company	192.20	576.60
Medicare Company	44.95	134.85
Federal Unemployment	4.80	42.00
OH - Unemployment Comp...	83.70	251.10

Check Amount: 2,508.31

Save & Previous   **K** Save & Next   **L** Save & Close   Cancel   Help   ☐ Enter net/Calculate gross

Confirmation and Next Steps

① Enter Payroll Information   ② Review & Create Paychecks   ③ **Print & Distribute Paychecks**

✓ **You have successfully created 3 paychecks:**

3 handwritten checks   **0** for direct deposit   Learn more

Next step:

Print your paychecks/stubs, and distribute to employees.

[Print Paychecks]   [Print Pay Stubs]

N Close

Prepare a General Journal Entry

The General Journal Entry window is used to prepare general journal entries that are not entered during the normal course of business. The accounts in the general ledger are updates with a debit, and a credit is also made from the journal entry.

Transactions	DR	CR	Subsidiary Records Updated	General Ledger Updated
Appropriate Account or Accounts	$		✓	✓
Appropriate Account or Accounts		$	✓	✓

Quick Reference Table

Step	Box or Other Location	Procedure
A	Home Page	Click the Company menu and select Make General Journal Entries. *Note:* If a window opens with information about automatic journal entry numbering, click OK.
B	Date	Accept default date or change.
C	Entry No.	Accept default journal entry number or change.
D	Account	Select an account to be debited from the drop-down list.
E	Debit	Enter the amount to be debited.
F	Memo	Briefly type a description of the journal entry.
G	Name	Select the appropriate customer, vendor, or employee, if applicable.
H	Debit	Repeat steps E–G for additional debits.
I	Account	Select an account to be credited from the drop-down list.
J	Credit	Enter the amount to be credited to the account selected in step I.
K	Name	Select the appropriate customer, vendor, or employee, if applicable.
L	Credit	Repeat steps I through K for additional credits.
M	Make General Journal Entries window	Review the information to verify that it is correct.
N	Save & Close / Save & New buttons	Click the Save & Close or Save & New button.

Prepare a General Journal Entry
QuickBooks windows

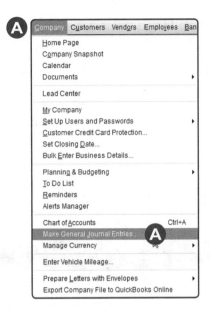

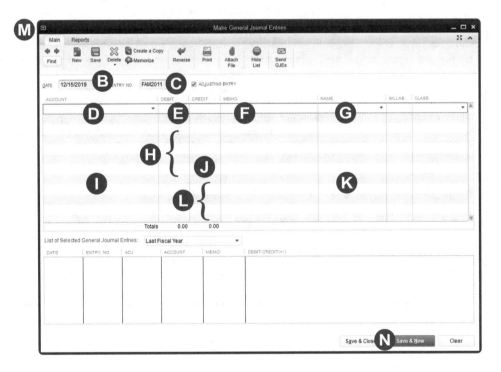

Adjust Perpetual Inventory Records

The Adjust Quantity/Value on Hand window allows users to adjust their inventory records.

Transactions	DR		CR	Subsidiary Records Updated	General Ledger Updated
Cost of Goods Sold	$	or	$		✓
Inventory	$	or	$	✓	✓

Quick Reference Table

Step	Box or Other Location	Procedure
A	Home Page	Click the drop-down arrow next to the Inventory Activities icon under Company.
B	Inventory Activities drop-down list *(not shown)*	Select Adjust Quantity/Value On Hand.
C	Adjustment Type	Select Quantity from the drop-down list if it is not already selected.
D	Adjustment Date	Accept default date or edit.
E	Adjustment Account	Select the account that will be adjusted from the drop-down list *(not shown)*. If a message appears titled Income or Expense expected, click the "Do not display this message again" box and click OK.
F	Item	Select the item to be adjusted.
G	New Quantity	Enter the correct quantity.
H	Various	Repeat steps F and G for each inventory item being adjusted.
I	Adjust Quantity/ Value on Hand window	Verify the information entered.
J	Save & Close	Click the Save & Close button.

Adjust Perpetual Inventory Records
QuickBooks windows

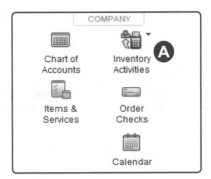

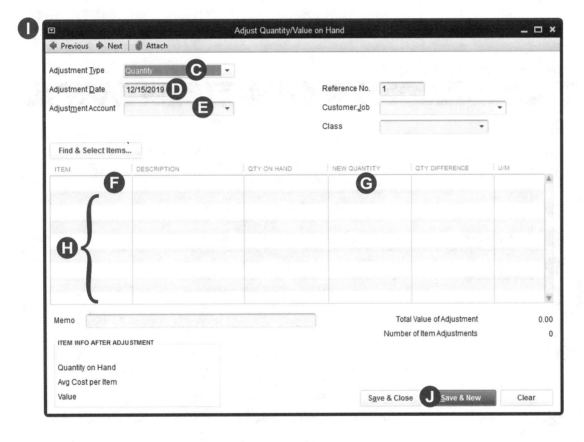

Prepare a Bank Reconciliation

The Reconciliation Window allows the user to prepare periodic bank reconciliations.

Transactions	DR		CR	Subsidiary Records Updated	General Ledger Updated
Appropriate Bank Account	$	or	$		✓
Other Appropriate Accounts	$	or	$		✓
Bank Service Charge	$				✓
Interest Income			$		✓

Quick Reference Table

Step	Box or Other Location	Procedure
A	Home Page	Click the Reconcile icon under Banking.
B	Account	Select an account from the drop-down list to be reconciled.
C	Statement Date	Accept the default date or edit.
D	Ending Balance	Enter the correct ending balance.
E	Service Charge	Enter the amount charged.
F	Date	Accept the default date or edit.
G	Account	Select the appropriate general ledger account for the service charge from the drop-down list.
H	Interest Earned	Enter the correct amount of interest earned.
I	Date	Accept the default date or edit.
J	Account	Select the appropriate general ledger account for the interest revenue from the drop-down list.
K	Continue	Select the Continue button to proceed to the Reconcile window.
L	Hide transactions checkbox	Click the "Hide transactions after the statement's end date" checkbox so that only transactions through the bank statement ending date are shown in the window.
M	Various	For each item cleared with the bank statement, click anywhere on that item's line to indicate the item is no longer outstanding.
N	Reconcile window	Review the information to verify that it is correct.
O	Reconcile Now	Click the Reconcile Now button.
P	Select Reconciliation Report window (not shown)	Click the Display button to preview the bank reconciliation. If you want to print a copy after previewing it, use the Print button.

Prepare a Bank Reconciliation

QuickBooks windows

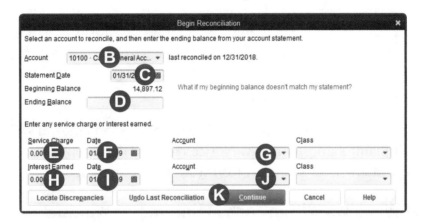

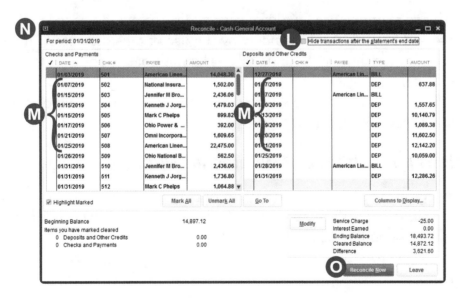

Perform Maintenance Activities

There are five types of maintenance in this project. The purposes of maintenance for each type are to (1) add, (2) change, or (3) delete default information for the five maintenance windows. Information that is changed through maintenance can be categorized into two types:

1. Information that makes it easier to record transactions. An example is information in a drop-down list to identify customers.

2. Information that directly affects the amounts recorded in subsequent transactions. Examples include a change in the unit selling price of a product and a pay rate increase for an employee.

In addition to the maintenance tasks described above, other areas of *QuickBooks* involve maintenance. For example, setting up a new company in *QuickBooks* requires knowledge of most maintenance windows and tasks. Chapter 10 provides instructions and practice for setting up a new company.

Accessing a Maintenance Window

The second column in the table on page 59 shows the sequence of steps necessary to access each maintenance window. Notice that the first step in accessing each maintenance window is to select an icon from the Home Page.

Additional Windows Within Each Maintenance Window

Three of the five maintenance windows have additional windows (sub-windows) that are accessed from the main window by the use of tabs. Inventory and General Ledger maintenance windows have no tabs. The main tab is shown for these three maintenance windows when the main window is first opened. The sub-windows contain additional information related to the main maintenance window. Only certain sub-windows are used in the project.

Instructions for Each Type of Maintenance Window

Instructions for using each of the five types of maintenance windows is explained in a section that follows. Each section contains window illustrations, along with reference tables for adding, changing, and deleting a record. The Quick Reference Table on the facing page identifies the Reference book page numbers for each type of maintenance.

Perform Maintenance Activities

Quick Reference Table

Maintenance Window Name	Steps Necessary to Access Maintenance Window	Functions Performed by Maintenance Window
Customer Maintenance (pages 60–63)	**Add a new record:** *Click the Customers icon → Customers & Jobs tab → New Customer & Job button → New Customer.* **Change a record or delete a record:** *Click the Customers icon → Customers & Jobs tab → right-click on any customer → Edit Customer: Job or Delete Customer: Job.*	Used to add a new customer, view and/or change data for an existing customer, or delete a former customer.
Vendor Maintenance (pages 64–67)	**Add a new record:** *Click the Vendors icon → Vendors Tab → New Vendor button → New Vendor* **Change a record or delete a record:** *Click the Vendors icon → Vendors tab → right-click on any vendor → select Edit Vendor or Delete Vendor.*	Used to add a new vendor, view and/or change data for a vendor on file, or delete a former vendor.
Inventory Item Maintenance (pages 68–72)	*Click the Items & Services icon → right-click on any item → select New, Edit Item, or Delete Item.*	Used to add a new inventory item, view and/or change existing information, or delete an item no longer being purchased or sold.
Employee Maintenance (pages 74–80)	**Add a new record:** *Click the Employees icon → Employees Tab → New Employee button.* **Change a record or delete a record:** *Click the Employees icon → Employees tab → right-click on any employee → select Edit Employee or Delete Employee.*	Used to add a new employee, view and/or change existing employee information, or delete a former employee.
General Ledger Account Maintenance (pages 82–85)	*Click the Chart of Accounts icon → right-click on any account → select New, Edit Account, or Delete Account.*	Used to add a new general ledger account, view and/or change data for an account on file, or delete an account no longer being used.

Customer Maintenance

The table below and the two tables on the following page include instructions to add a customer record, change information for an existing customer, and delete a former customer's record. The *QuickBooks* windows for these maintenance activities are shown on pages 62 and 63.

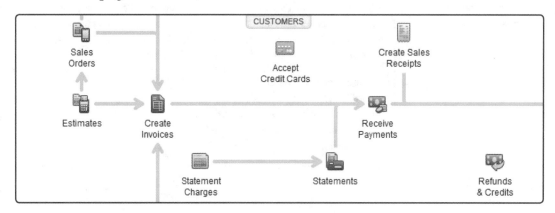

Add a Customer Record
Quick Reference Table

Box or Other Location	Procedure
Home Page	Click the Customers icon to display the Customer Center.
Customers & Jobs Tab	Click the Customers & Jobs tab if it is not already open.
New Customer & Job button	Click the New Customer & Job button. Select New Customer to open the New Customer window.
Customer Name	Enter the name of the customer.
Opening Balance	Do not enter. Will be done later if there is a balance.
As of	Enter date the customer is added.
Remainder of Address Info tab	Complete the remaining boxes to the extent that the information is available. Some boxes may not be applicable for the customer. For the Address Details section, you can use the Copy button if the Ship To address is the same as the Invoice/Bill To address.
Payment Settings tab	Select the Payment Settings tab. Complete the boxes to the extent that the information is available. Some boxes may not be applicable for the customer.
Sales Tax Settings tab	Select the Sales Tax Settings tab. Complete the boxes to the extent that the information is available. Some boxes may not be applicable for the customer.
OK button	Click the OK button to save the new customer information and close the window.

Change Information in An Existing Customer's Record
Quick Reference Table

Box or Other Location	Procedure
Home Page	Click the Customers icon to display the Customer Center.
Customer Center	Click the Customers & Jobs tab to display the customer list.
Customer List	Right-click on the customer name that is to be changed and select Edit Customer: Job to open the Edit Customer window.
Edit Customer window	Change appropriate information in the windows for the Address Info, Payment Settings, and Sales Tax Settings tabs.
OK button	Click the OK button to save the edited customer information and close the window.

Delete a Former Customer's Record
Quick Reference Table

Box or Other Location	Procedure
Home Page	Click the Customers icon to display the Customer Center.
Customer Center	Click the Customers & Jobs tab to display the customer list.
Customer List	Right-click on the customer name that is to be deleted and select Delete Customer: Job. (*Note:* Be sure you want to delete the customer record before you do so. If you want that customer included later, you will need to find and reenter the information as you would for a new customer following the guidance in Add a Customer Record – Quick Reference Table.) Click OK to delete the customer, or click Cancel if you choose not to delete the customer.
QuickBooks message	If the account is associated with at least one transaction in the current year or has a prior balance, a warning message will appear. Either click Cancel to cancel the attempted deletion or click the Make Inactive button. If you choose to inactivate the customer, click Yes if you receive a message saying that the customer has an outstanding balance. Making a customer inactive only eliminates that customer from view when Active Customers are shown in QuickBooks. It does not delete the customer entirely.

Customer Maintenance

QuickBooks windows

Customer Center → Customers & Jobs Tab →
New Customer & Job → New Customer

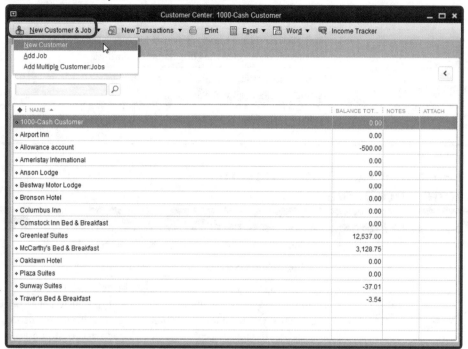

New Customer Window—Address Info Tab

(windows continued on the following page)

Customer Maintenance

QuickBooks windows *(continued)*

New Customer Window—Payment Settings Tab

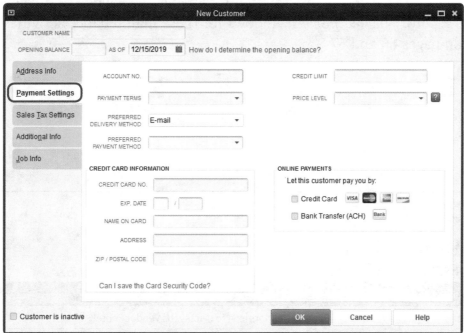

New Customer Window—Sales Tax Settings Tab

Vendor Maintenance

The table below and the two tables on the following page include instructions to add a vendor record, change information for an existing vendor, and delete a former vendor's record. The *QuickBooks* windows for these maintenance activities are shown on pages 66 and 67.

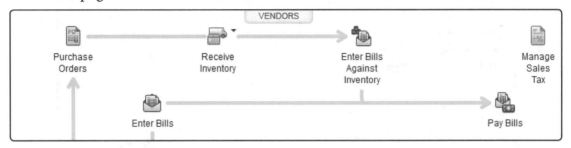

Add a Vendor Record
Quick Reference Table

Box or Other Location	Procedure
Home Page	Click the Vendors icon to display the Vendor Center.
Vendors Tab	Click the Vendors tab if it is not already open.
New Vendor button	Click the New Vendor button. Select New Vendor to open the New Vendor window.
Vendor Name	Enter the name of the vendor.
Opening Balance	Do not enter. Will be done later if there is a balance.
As of	Enter date the vendor is added.
Remainder of Address Info tab	Complete the remaining boxes to the extent that the information is available. Some boxes may not be applicable for the vendor.
Payment Settings tab	Select the Payment Settings tab. Complete the boxes to the extent that the information is available. Some boxes may not be applicable for the vendor.
Account Settings tab	Select the Account Settings tab. Enter the general ledger account(s) that purchases from this vendor are likely to be charged to.
OK button	Click the OK button to save the new vendor information and close the window.

Change Information in An Existing Vendor's Record
Quick Reference Table

Box or Other Location	Procedure
Home Page	Click the Vendors icon to display the Vendor Center.
Vendor Center	Click the Vendors tab to display the vendor list.
Vendor List	Right-click on the name of the vendor whose record you wish to change and select Edit Vendor to open the Edit Vendor window.
Edit Vendor window	Change appropriate information in the windows for the Address Info, Payment Settings, and/or Account Settings tabs.
OK button	Click the OK button to save the edited vendor information and close the window.

Delete a Former Vendor's Record
Quick Reference Table

Box or Other Location	Procedure
Home Page	Click the Vendors tab to display the Vendor Center.
Vendor Center	Click the Vendors tab to display the vendor list.
Vendor List	Right-click on the vendor name that is to be deleted and select Delete Vendor. (*Note:* Be sure you want to delete the vendor record before you do so. If you want that vendor included later, you will need to find and reenter the information as you would for a new vendor following the guidance in Add a Vendor Record–Quick Reference Table.)
QuickBooks message	If the account is associated with at least one transaction in the current year or has a prior balance, a warning message will appear. For this project, click cancel and do not delete the account.

Vendor Maintenance
QuickBooks windows

Vendor Center → Vendors Tab → New Vendor button → New Vendor

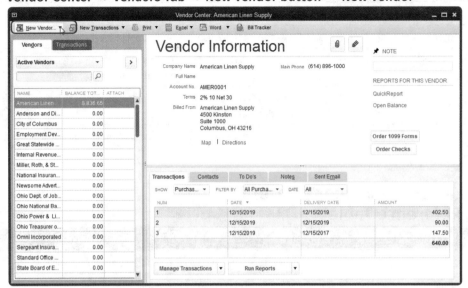

New Vendor Window—Address Info Tab

(windows continued on the following page)

Vendor Maintenance

QuickBooks windows *(continued)*

New Vendor Window—Payment Settings Tab

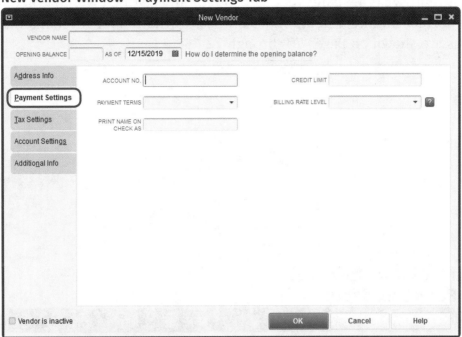

New Vendor Window—Account Settings Tab

Inventory Item Maintenance

The table below and the two tables on the following page include instructions to add an inventory item, change information for an existing inventory item, and delete a former inventory item. The *QuickBooks* windows for these maintenance activities are shown on pages 70 through 72.

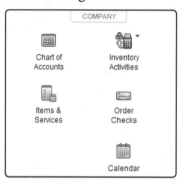

Add an Inventory Item Record
Quick Reference Table

Box or Other Location	Procedure
Home Page	Click the Items & Services icon on the right under Company to open the Item List window *(not shown)*.
Item List window	Right-click on any inventory item on the list and click New to open the New Item window.
New Item window	Select Inventory Part from the drop-down list under Type.
Item Name/Number	Enter the item name and/or number.
Purchase Information	Complete the boxes in the Purchase Information section to the extent that the information is available. Some boxes may not be applicable for the inventory item.
Sales Information	Complete the boxes in the Sales Information section to the extent that the information is available. Some boxes may not be applicable for the inventory item.
Inventory Information	Complete the boxes in the Inventory Information section to the extent that the information is available. Some boxes may not be applicable for the inventory item.
OK button	Click the OK button to save the new item information and close the window.

Change Information in An Existing Inventory Item's Record
Quick Reference Table

Box or Other Location	Procedure
Home Page	Click the Items & Services icon.
Item List window	Right-click on the inventory item that is to be changed and select Edit Item to open the Edit Item window.
Edit Item window	Change the appropriate information in the window.
OK button	Click the OK button to save the edited inventory information and close the window.

Delete an Inventory Item No Longer Being Purchased or Sold
Quick Reference Table

Box or Other Location	Procedure
Home Page	Click the Items & Services icon.
Item List	Right-click on the item that is to be deleted and select Delete Item. (*Note:* Be sure you want to delete the inventory item before you do so. If you want that inventory item included later, you will need to find and reenter the information as you would for a new inventory item following the guidance in Add an Inventory Item Record – Quick Reference Table.)
QuickBooks message	If the inventory item is associated with at least one transaction in the current year or has quantities in the inventory item, a warning message will appear. The message will inform you that the item cannot be deleted. For this project, click cancel and do not delete the item.

Inventory Item Maintenance

QuickBooks windows

New Item Window—Type

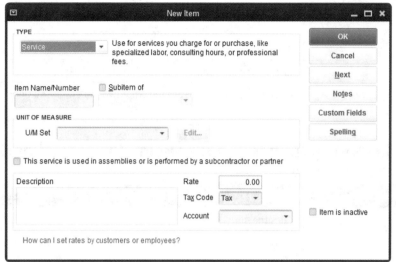

New Item Window—Type → Inventory Part

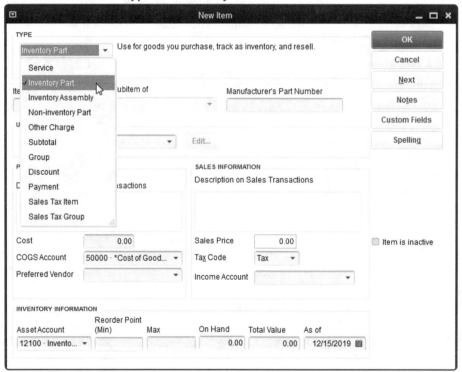

(windows continued on the following page)

Reference—Payroll Cycle and Other Activities

Inventory Item Maintenance

QuickBooks **windows** *(continued)*

New Item Window—Item Name / Number

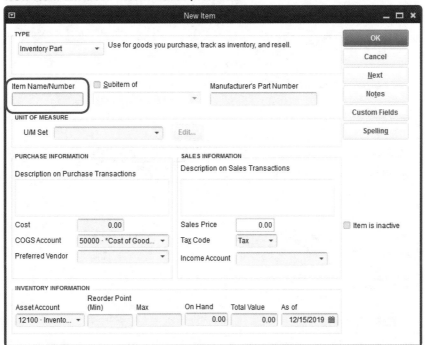

New Item Window—Purchase Information

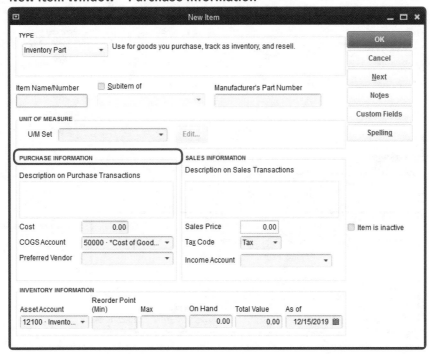

(windows continued on the following page)

Inventory Item Maintenance

QuickBooks **windows** *(continued)*

New Item Window—Sales Information

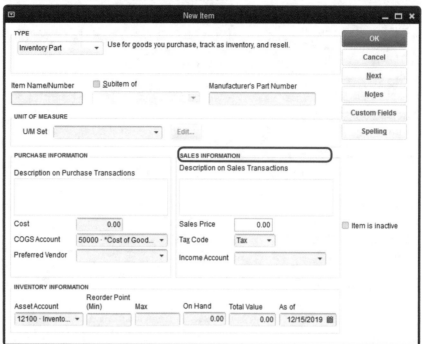

New Item Window—Inventory Information

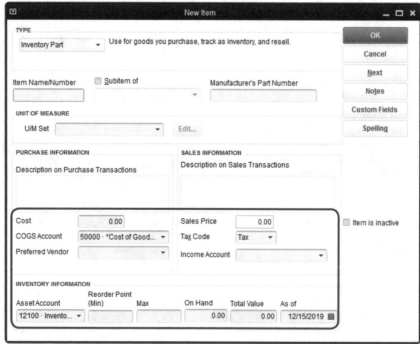

This page is intentionally blank.

Employee Maintenance

The table below and the two tables on the following page include instructions to add an employee, change information for an existing employee, and delete a former employee. The *QuickBooks* windows for these maintenance activities are shown on pages 76 through 80.

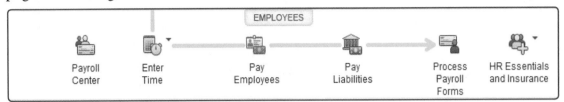

Add an Employee Record
Quick Reference Table

Box or Other Location	Procedure
Home Page	Click the Employees icon to display the Employee Center.
Employees Tab	Click the Employees tab if it is not already open.
New Employee button	Click the New Employee button to open the New Employee window.
Personal tab	Complete the boxes to the extent that the information is available. Some boxes may not be applicable for the employee.
Address & Contact tab	Select the Address & Contact tab. Complete the boxes to the extent that the information is available. Some boxes may not be applicable for the employee.
Additional Info tab	Select the Additional Info tab. Enter the employee account number, if applicable.
Employment Info tab	Select the Employment Info tab. Enter the hire date.
Payroll Info tab	Select the Payroll Info tab. Enter the pay frequency, then enter the salary, hourly, and/or overtime amounts/rates into the Earnings section of the window. Click the Taxes button.
Federal tab	Complete the boxes to the extent that information is available, including exemptions.
State tab	Select the State Worked and the State Subject to Withholding from the drop-down menu. Enter the number of allowances.
Other tab	Use this tab to Add new payroll item such as surcharges, contributions, or other User-Defined taxes.
OK button	Click the OK button to save the entered employee information and close the window.

Change Information in An Existing Employee's Record
Quick Reference Table

Box or Other Location	Procedure
Home Page	Click the Employees icon to display the Employee Center.
Employee Center	Click the Employees tab to display the employee list.
Employee List	Right-click on the employee name that is to be changed and select Edit Employee to open the Edit Employee window.
Edit Employee window	Choose the relevant tab(s). Change appropriate information in the windows.
OK button	Click the OK button to save the edited employee information and close the window.

Delete a Former Employee's Record
Quick Reference Table

Box or Other Location	Procedure
Home Page	Click the Employees icon to display the Employee Center.
Employee Center	Click the Employees tab to display the employee list.
Name column	Right-click on the employee name that is to be deleted and select Delete Employee. (*Note:* Be sure you want to delete the employee record before you do so. If you want that employee included later, you will need to find and reenter the information as you would for a new employee following the guidance in Add an Employee Record – Quick Reference Table.)
QuickBooks message	If the employee is associated with at least one transaction in the current year or has a prior balance, a warning message will appear. For this project, click cancel and do not delete the employee.

Employee Maintenance
QuickBooks windows

Employee Center → Employees Tab → New Employee

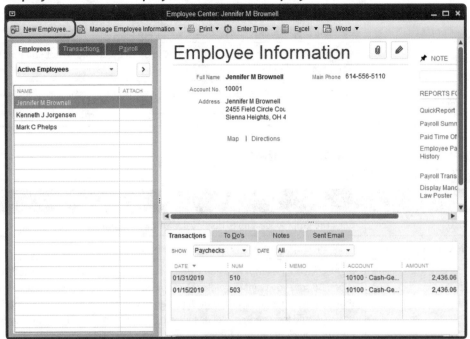

New Employee Window—Personal Tab

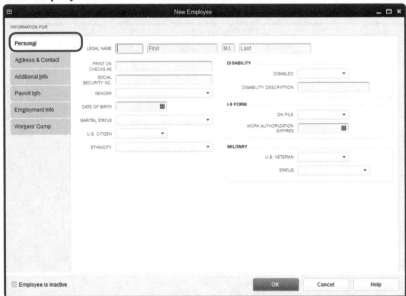

(windows continued on the following page)

Reference—Payroll Cycle and Other Activities

Employee Maintenance

QuickBooks **windows** *(continued)*

New Employee Window—Address & Contact Tab

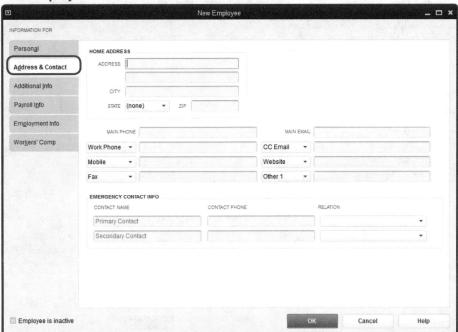

New Employee Window—Additional Info Tab

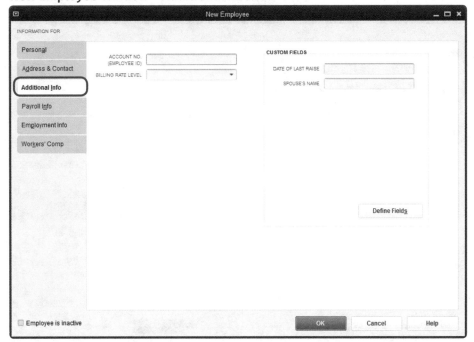

(windows continued on the following page)

Employee Maintenance

QuickBooks **windows** *(continued)*

New Employee Window—Employment Info Tab

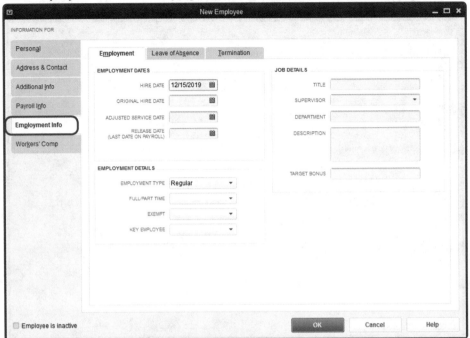

New Employee Window—Payroll Info Tab

(windows continued on the following page)

Reference—Payroll Cycle and Other Activities

Employee Maintenance

QuickBooks **windows** *(continued)*

Taxes Window—Federal Tab

Taxes Window—State Tab

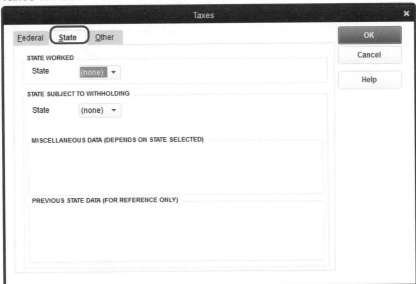

(windows continued on the following page)

Employee Maintenance

QuickBooks windows *(continued)*

Taxes Window—Other Tab

This page is intentionally blank.

General Ledger Account Maintenance

The table below and the two tables on the following page include instructions to add a general ledger account, change information for an existing general ledger account, and delete a former general ledger account. The *QuickBooks* windows for these maintenance activities are shown on pages 84 and 85.

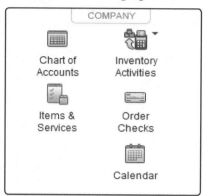

Add a General Ledger Account Record
Quick Reference Table

Box or Other Location	Procedure
Home Page	Click the Chart of Accounts icon to open the Chart of Accounts window.
Chart of Accounts window	Right-click on any chart of accounts name and select New.
Add New Account: Choose Account Type window	Select the type of account being created and click the Continue button.
Number	Enter the account number.
Account Name	Enter account name.
Description	Enter a description of the new account, if appropriate.
Tax-Line Mapping	Accept default entry or change based on information given for the new account.
Save & Close / Save & New buttons	Click the Save & Close or Save & New button to save the account created.

Change Information in An Existing General Ledger Account's Record Quick Reference Table

Box or Other Location	Procedure
Home Page	Click the Chart of Accounts icon to open the Chart of Accounts window.
List of Accounts	Right-click on the account name that is to be changed and select Edit Account to open the Edit Account window.
Edit Account window	Change appropriate information in the window.
Save & Close button	Click the Save & Close button to save the edited account information and close the window.

Delete a General Ledger Account Record No Longer Being Used Quick Reference Table

Box or Other Location	Procedure
Home Page	Click the Chart of Accounts icon to open the Chart of Accounts window.
List of Accounts	Right-click on the account name that is to be deleted and select Delete Account. (*Note:* Be sure you want to delete the account before you do so. If you want that account included later, you will need to find and reenter the information as you would for a new account following the guidance in Add a General Ledger Account Record – Quick Reference Table.)
QuickBooks message	If the account is associated with at least one transaction in the current year or has a prior balance, a warning message will appear. For this project, click cancel and do not delete the account.

General Ledger Account Maintenance

QuickBooks windows

Chart of Accounts Window → New

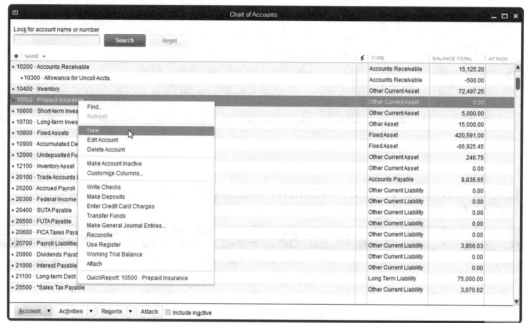

Add New Account—Choose Account Type Window

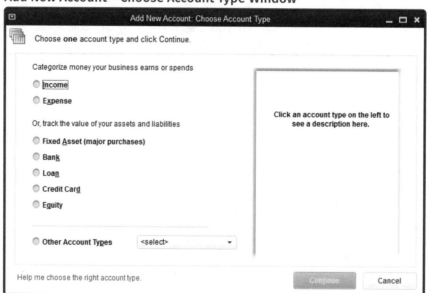

(windows continued on the following page)

General Ledger Account Maintenance

QuickBooks **windows** *(continued)*

Add New Account Window

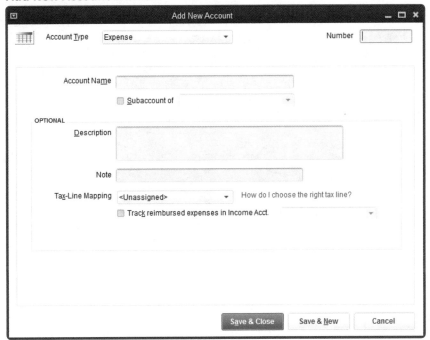

A R M O N D 𝒜 D A L T O N

2867 Jolly Road
Okemos, Michigan 48864-3547

517-351-8520 (t)
517-351-8590 (f)

adpub@armonddalton.com
armonddalton.com

ISBN 978-0-912503-71-4

ISBN 978-0-912503-71-4

9 780912 503714